Jackson Nieuwland

Published in 2018 by The Rosen Publishing Group, Inc.
29 East 21st Street, New York, NY 10010

Library of Congress Cataloging-in-Publication Data

Names: Nieuwland, Jackson, author.
Title: Coping with social media anxiety / Jackson Nieuwland.
Description: New York : Rosen, 2018 | Series: Coping |
Audience: Grades 7–12. | Includes bibliographical references and index.
Identifiers: LCCN 2017014246 | ISBN 9781508176978 (library bound) | ISBN 9781508178545 (paperback)
Subjects: LCSH: Anxiety. | Social media — Psychological aspects.
Classification: LCC BF575.A6 N54 2018 | DDC 152.4/6 — dc23
LC record available at https://lccn.loc.gov/2017014246

Manufactured in China

CONTENTS

INTRODUCTION

Rowan Young and three other people liked your photo.
Alex Nelson tagged you in a post.
Jayden Langston invited you to like his page What We Talk About.
Blake Lee and four others have birthdays today.
Jordan Yu invited you to This Is Actually a Party.
Micah Sands mentioned you in a comment.
Morgan Espinosa posted in Cool Dog Group.
Shiloh O'Connor added a new photo.

Sometimes all those notifications from social media just become too much. It's stressful to try and keep up with everything that's going on. How are you supposed to stay up to date with everything your friends are doing online, read all the articles to which people are linking, and do your homework? Occasionally, it gets to the point where you can't bear to look at social media at all. Then of course you forget to post happy birthday on someone's timeline and he or she might get really upset with you.

@girlsjustwannahavefood reblogged your photo and added: "That's an incredible sandwich."
@krisbarnes liked your quote.
@besttodolists liked your post: To Do Today.
@alphabetasoupa is following

@theendofthebeginningoftheend.
@stupidpicturesofmygoldfish is a genius.
@newmoonfriend started following you.
@dogzrbetterthangodz reblogged your post:

Trying to get anything at all done when your phone is constantly buzzing with messages from all your social media accounts can be overwhelming.

Who Needs Love When You Could Have…
@jojomojo gave this post some love.

Other times you stress out about not getting enough validation on social media. *Why hasn't Jamie reacted to my relationship status? Why didn't Sam tag me in that photo?* You think you feel your phone buzzing, but when you check it there's nothing there. You notice that you've lost a follower on Instagram and scroll through, trying to figure out who it is and why he or she unfollowed you. Are you posting too many photos of your cat, or did he or she just follow you so that you would follow him or her back? These are the sorts of things you can spend hours obsessing over.

@oceanofhorses liked your Tweet: I want to go home even when I'm at home.
@sadversionofmel added you to the list Sad People Who Are Also Funny.
@tinytinyant is now following you!
Mentioned by @sugaruniversity: @socialmediaanxiety saaaaame
@theoneandonly Tweeted: Just scored tickets to Beyonce!!!!
@al_masters Retweeted a Tweet you were mentioned in: @socialmediaanxiety is the…
@p_blqck and @jayjaydemario are talking about the musician Lorde.

@gerrylamonte Retweeted your Retweet: Can't wait till the world just transforms into a giant turtle.

If you can relate to any of this, there's a chance you're experiencing social media anxiety. And it's not just you. There are millions of people out there dealing with the exact same problems, trying to balance social media with the rest of their lives, feeling stressed and overwhelmed. It can be difficult to handle, but the good news is, there are plenty of ways to cope with social media anxiety. You just have to figure out which ones are best for you.

CHAPTER ONE

What Does Social Media Have to Do with Anxiety?

Social media is an inescapable part of modern life. It's connected to so many of the things we do on a daily basis, from eating meals to going to work. Although social media brings a lot of people pleasure and fulfillment, some people find that social media has a negative effect on their well-being, causing them stress and worry. These people experience something called social media anxiety, a new phenomena that researchers are still learning more about, but which affects millions of people around the world.

What Is Social Media?

Everyone knows what social media is. Even if you don't use it, you can't avoid it. There are tweets on

Most people bring their phones with them everywhere, so social media is always just an arm's reach away.

the news, people posting Facebook statuses on the bus, and countless emails from LinkedIn in your inbox. You can probably name ten social media platforms off the top of your head: Facebook, Twitter, Instagram, Pinterest, Snapchat, Tumblr, Google+, LinkedIn, MySpace, Ello. But actually defining social media is more difficult than you might think, especially because new social media platforms are launching all the time, each one potentially expanding the limits of how social media can be defined.

Every social media platform has a different set of features, so how do we decide what it is that makes a website or an app a form of social media? Is YouTube social media? What about Reddit? In order to create a definition of social media, we need to determine what these platforms have in common: they are based online, you need an account to use them, you can use your account to connect

If you have a smartphone, it's hard to avoid social media. After all, Facebook is the Apple App Store's most downloaded app, with Instagram and Twitter close behind.

with other users, and the content on the platform is generated by the users.

So social media can be broadly defined as platforms that allow the sharing of user-generated content through profile-based online networks. Or more simply put: websites or apps where you can sign in and share things with your friends.

Although it may not seem like it now, social media actually hasn't been around for all that long. The first social media website was called SixDegrees (based on the six degrees of separation concept). It was launched in 1997 and allowed users to create an account; list their friends, family members, and acquaintances; message them; and post on their pages. But it wasn't until 2003 that social media really took off with the launch of MySpace. In addition to allowing users to connect and communicate with their friends, MySpace had many other functions, such as blogging, the ability to embed music and video to your profile page, and an ability to rank your top eight friends. MySpace was the most popular social media platform for several years, until it was overtaken by newer platforms for which it had paved the way like Facebook and Twitter. Now those platforms, which began as websites but are now available as smartphone apps, are facing even newer competition from platforms like Snapchat and

Instagram. Who knows what the next social media platform to take over will be.

What Is Anxiety?

Anxiety is an emotion that everyone experiences. It is a feeling of worry, stress, or inner turmoil about a future event. Although this might seem similar to fear, there is an important difference between the two. Fear is triggered by an immediate, objective danger, whereas anxiety is based in anticipation. It comes from thinking about things that might happen or go wrong and is often more long lasting than fear. For instance, you would feel fear if a car was speeding toward you with no sign of stopping, but you would feel anxious if you worried about being hit by a car every time you crossed the street.

Anxiety is not a mental disorder on its own, but it is a symptom of many mental disorders, and many mental disorders have the word "anxiety" in their names, such as social anxiety disorder and general anxiety disorder. In fact, according to the National Institute of Mental Health, 18 percent of Americans older than eighteen experience anxiety disorders, making them the most common form of mental illness in the United States. Not only that but the average

Julie Spira may get invited to walk the red carpet, but that has nothing to do with being a qualified psychologist.

age of onset is eleven years old, meaning that these disorders can continue for years, from childhood into adulthood.

Although the term "social media anxiety disorder" is used by some people to describe social media anxiety, this term was coined by Julie Spira, an online dating expert who does not have a degree in psychology, and is not a recognized clinical condition. This is not to say that social media anxiety is not a serious issue or that it won't one day be classified as a mental disorder; it just shows that it is still a developing area of study, and you need to make sure you're getting your information from credible sources. If you think you are suffering from an anxiety disorder, you should seek the opinion of a qualified medical professional, because all cases are different, and they cannot always be correctly diagnosed without expert advice.

How Does Social Media Cause Anxiety?

So how do networks designed to help you keep in touch with your friends cause so much turmoil that people are coming up with medical terms for the phenomena? Well, the answer varies from person to person. No one's experience is exactly the same as anyone else's, but there are three main factors that contribute to social media anxiety: fear of missing out, overstimulation, and low

When you're experiencing anxiety, it can feel as if there is too much going on in your head for you to handle.

self-esteem. In some cases social media magnifies a problem someone already has; in others it triggers something that hadn't existed previously.

Fear of Missing Out (FOMO)

"Fear of missing out" (FOMO) is a term born on the internet, and while it doesn't only apply to social media it does contribute significantly to social media anxiety. Social media has become one of the main ways people keep up to date with the world around them. Not only can it be used to stay in touch with friends but it is also a news source, a way to plan and invite people to events, a place to search for jobs and accommodation, and much more. Users of social media often feel a need to keep checking their feeds in order to make sure they don't miss anything important, and when they don't have access to social media, they sometimes feel anxious that there might be something happening on social media that they should be seeing. *What if one of my friends announces she's in a relationship while I'm camping without Wi-Fi?*

It's hard to resist the temptation to check in on social media, no matter how interesting the book you're reading is.

The problem is that it is physically impossible to keep up with everything that happens online—there's just too much of it—and so it's also impossible not to be missing out on something. So basically, you can feel anxious that you're missing out on something on social media even when you're on social media. FOMO leads people to use social media more and more often to avoid missing out. Then of course this causes more problems.

Not only do people worry about missing out on things that happen on social media but when they're on social media, they worry about missing out on the events their friends are posting about having attended. When they see photos of their friends going to the movies together, they wonder why they weren't invited and what else they've been left out of. Most of the time these sorts of exclusions are not malicious; maybe your schedule didn't fit with your friends that day or perhaps they just needed a one-

on-one catch up, but because the posts about them are accessible online, it can seem like people are flaunting them. Try to remember that this isn't necessarily the case.

Overstimulation

When we sign into our social media accounts, we are bombarded with information. The Real Time Statistics Project reports that on average, six thousand tweets are posted on Twitter every second, more than three million photos are shared on Instagram every hour, and fifty-five million status updates are made on Facebook every day. And people aren't even just looking at one social media platform at a time. Tabbed browsing allows people to quickly click between multiple websites. In less than a minute someone could go from scrolling through Pinterest to filming a Snapchat to checking his or her Facebook notifications. This is more than the human brain is designed to cope with.

When people are browsing social media on their phones or computers, they are often doing something else at the same time, whether it's listening to music, watching television, writing an essay, or having a conversation. This is what is called multitasking. Unfortunately, humans aren't wired to multitask. What people

It's not uncommon to be scrolling through Pinterest on your laptop and then hear your phone buzzing with a notification from Snapchat, which you absolutely have to check right now.

are actually doing in these situations is switching back and forth between tasks very quickly, and this takes a toll.

Trying to juggle these different tasks actually changes people's brain chemistry. So-called multitasking causes increased levels of cortisol (the stress hormone) and adrenaline (the fight-or-flight hormone), which can overstimulate the brain, causing erratic thoughts. Sounds like the perfect recipe for anxiety.

Low Self-Esteem

Low self-esteem was a problem long before the invention of social media and it will continue to be a problem in the unlikely scenario that we stop using social media altogether. But for people with low self-esteem, social media can be an extremely damaging place. It can also foster low self-esteem in people who were previously very confident in themselves.

The connection between social media and low self-esteem is rooted in the way people compare themselves to others online. Social media provides users with more access than ever before into other peoples' lives. They see their friends hanging out without them, cooking delicious meals, and falling in love; their workmates going on exotic holidays, buying new cars, and celebrating promotions; and celebrities going to the gym, wearing expensive clothing, and

attending exclusive events. People inevitably compare themselves to these posts that they see online. What they don't always realize is that this isn't a fair comparison.

People curate their social media presences as a way to present the best possible version of themselves. Most of the time they only share things online that they think are impressive or funny. They will post the photo of them relaxing on the beach in their new swimsuits, but not the seven others where the straps are bursting open, the wind is blowing sand all over them, and their hair is out of control. So when people compare themselves to their friends on social media, they are judging themselves against an impossible standard, because they are comparing themselves in their current state against their friends at their very best. That's bound to make anyone feel bad about himself or herself.

When you're feeling bad about not measuring up to what your friends are posting online, remember this: they're trying to make themselves look good because they're insecure, too. The primary reason people only post the most flattering content on social media is that they want to make themselves look better than they think they are. They probably feel like they don't measure up to what you're posting yourself.

This cycle of low self-esteem is fueled by the design of these platforms. Most social media platforms have a

What seems like a spontaneous moment in a photo posted online is more often than not carefully planned and posed.

"like" or "favorite" feature. People judge the value of their posts (and therefore themselves) on how many likes they receive. This results in users basing their self-worth on external praise. It is a volatile way to assess yourself, because you have no control over how many people like your posts. Sure, you feel good when one of your selfies gets a lot of likes, but that feeling doesn't last. If your next post doesn't get the same response, you could be plunged into self-doubt.

Myths & FACTS

Myth: Things that happen online don't matter because they're not "real."

Fact: There are plenty of things that happen online that have real effects on people's lives. Just because someone says something to you online, rather than in person, doesn't mean it has any less effect on you. Of course, there are things online that are unimportant, but there are plenty of unimportant things going on offline as well. To suggest that cyberbullying, long-distance relationships, and online classes aren't "real" is ridiculous and disrespectful to the people who experience them. These things influence people's lives just as much as the things that happen to them offline.

Myth: People who post a lot of selfies are vain.

Fact: A 2016 study by Yongjun Sung found four core reasons why people post selfies online: attention seeking, communication, archiving, and entertainment. Of those four reasons, only attention seeking is linked to vanity. Plenty of people are sharing their selfies on social media because they find it fun or to document that they were doing something at a certain time. Also, the people who *are* posting selfies to get attention are often not doing so to show off but are actually trying to gain the validation or approval of their friends or peers, which is more or less the opposite of vanity.

Myth: Social media is a waste of time.

Fact: Although this resource is focused on one of the negative effects of social media, that doesn't mean that it doesn't have any positives. For many people, using social media is both enjoyable and fulfilling. Not only can people use social media to keep in touch with friends and family who live far away (which by the way is not a waste of time) but it is also a way to find jobs and housing, it's a valuable news source, and it's exceptionally useful in raising money for charities, all of which are immensely productive uses of one's time.

CHAPTER TWO

Do I Have Social Media Anxiety?

There's a good chance you're wondering if you have social media anxiety. It can often be difficult for people to recognize. Just because you spend a lot of time on social media doesn't mean you have social media anxiety. Just because you feel anxious and you also have a Pinterest account doesn't mean you have social media anxiety either. Unfortunately, because it isn't a recognized clinical condition, there is no established procedure for diagnosing social media anxiety. However, it is a pretty clear-cut concept: if social media causes you anxiety then you have social media anxiety. So if you think you have social media anxiety, then you probably do.

That being said, social media anxiety affects different people in different ways, and a lot of its symptoms are similar or identical to those of other anxiety disorders. Just because you don't experience all of the following symptoms doesn't mean you don't suffer from social media anxiety, but also just because you do experience some of them doesn't mean you necessarily have social media anxiety either. If you are concerned that you might have social media anxiety, consider talking to a doctor about it.

The following list of symptoms is by no means comprehensive. It is simply an outline of four of the most common and most recognizable symptoms. Hopefully, it will help you figure out whether you are experiencing social media anxiety and learn a bit more about how it is affecting you if you are.

Trouble Focusing

Often people experiencing social media anxiety feel anxious when they are unable to check social media. This feeling of anxiety can make it difficult to focus on other tasks. It's hard to write an essay when you're busy wondering how many likes the latest photo you shared on Instagram has gotten. And that's assuming you have the discipline not to check social media while you're writing the essay.

Modern society places a high value on multitasking. People are expected to be able to do multiple things at once. They're supposed to be able to read emails while they commute to work, answer the phone while they're in a meeting, and plan events while they eat their lunches, so it's no wonder we think we can browse social media while writing a paper. The only problem is that we can't actually do all these things at once, and it's not just because it's hard to focus on two or more things at the same time.

Multitasking creates what Daniel J. Levitin calls a "dopamine-addiction feedback loop," in which the brain is actually rewarded for losing focusing and searching for something new to pay attention to. This happens because multitasking is not actually doing multiple things at once but rather switching between different tasks very quickly. Whenever people switch to a new task their brains' prefrontal cortex releases a burst of endogenous opioids (brain chemicals that make you feel good), which is basically rewarding them for straying from the task at hand. And when they do stray, it is often to social media. It's easy to just tell yourself you'll just quickly check your notifications

Do you ever find yourself checking Facebook even when you know you should be doing something else? That's because social media is literally affecting your brain chemicals.

31

and get a quick blast of dopamine before continuing with your work, but it's hard to focus when your brain is literally working against you.

Even if you do manage to avoid the dangers of multitasking, the mere opportunity to check social media actually decreases your ability to focus. A study by psychiatrist Glenn Wilson found that when you are trying to focus on a task but are aware that there is an unread email waiting in your inbox, your IQ can be reduced by up to ten points. That's certainly going to stop you from being quite so productive.

Insomnia

Social media doesn't just cause sleep loss because people keep browsing late into the night (although this is a problem for some people). As with trouble focusing, social media causes insomnia through the effect it has on people's brains. The act of staring at a bright screen and concentrating on social media actually delays the brain's ability to get to sleep. This is because the screens of computers and phones emit a lot of blue light. Blue light signals to the brain that it is morning and time to wake up. The blue light suppresses melatonin, the hormone that regulates sleep. Usually people's melatonin levels rise right before bedtime, but this suppression results in people struggling to get to sleep, and even when they do get to sleep they are less likely

Try to avoid using your devices at night, especially when you're in bed. They could be the cause of your insomnia.

to reach REM sleep (the most restorative phase of the sleep cycle). If our screens emitted red light, however, they would actually help us get to sleep, because red light signals to the brain that it is evening.

Not only does social media affect our brain chemistry but it also has major effects on people's social expectations. Because of social media, people are now expected to be available twenty-four hours a day. So what if you're in bed in New York? It's morning in London and your friend has a question that needs to be answered right this minute. Giving in to this pressure to be accessible mean less sleep, but so does the stress of not giving into it. It can be hard to fall asleep when you're lying in bed just picturing the posts and messages piling up that will have to be dealt with next time you sign in, knowing that you'll have to apologize for the late response.

Even once you've gotten to sleep, you're not safe. Many people sleep with their phones within reach, especially those of us who use our phones as alarm clocks. Unfortunately, sometimes your phone can wake you earlier than you had planned. More and more often people are being woken in the night by notifications from social media, the light and buzzing from their phones disturbing their sleep. Also, when people wake during the night, perhaps needing to go to the bathroom or get a drink, there is the danger of them checking social media. Then they again run the risk of blue light tricking their brain into thinking that it's morning. It's a cycle of sleeplessness that's not doing anyone any favors.

Incessantly Checking Social Media

Yes, it seems obvious, but checking social media an unreasonable amount can be one of the most useful ways to realize that someone has a problem with social media. Although there are other possible causes for insomnia or for having trouble focusing, if you find yourself scrolling through Tumblr when someone is in the middle of telling you exciting news, it's pretty clear Tumblr has something to do with that lack of focus.

This compulsive use of social media can have a range of negative effects on people's lives. It can distract people from everyday tasks, which can be as minor as folding laundry or as high risk as driving to school. You don't want to be on Snapchat while you're driving on the highway. It can also damage personal relationships. Though the primary use of social media is to connect with other people, if you're still checking it while in the same room as friends, they could easily take offense, believing that you don't value their time

If you find yourself unable to take your eyes off your phone, even when you're crossing the street, it might be a sign you're addicted to social media.

or presence since you would rather be online, looking at social media.

Valuing social media over other forms of communication can often mean valuing surface-level interactions over deeper connections. It's much easier to like someone's Facebook status than to actually have a conversation with him about what's going on in his life. Though you may think you know people you have connected with through social media, the chances are that there are many things about them that they don't share online. A 2016 study by researchers from the Massachusetts Institute of Technology found that on average only 50 percent of the people someone considers his or her friends think of him or her in the same way.

Social media amplifies these types of false connections. It's easy to rack up hundreds or even thousands of "friends" without having to spend any time maintaining relationships with the people behind the profile pictures. According to evolutionary psychologist Robin I. M. Dunbar, people have layers of friendship. The highest layer can hold only a couple of people, perhaps a partner and a best friend, who you share more with than anyone else. The second layer can hold at most four people with whom you have strong relationships that require weekly upkeep. After that the layers hold more casual friends, so spending hours every day interacting with dozens of people online can mislead you into thinking you have more close friends than you really do and take time away from your most important relationships.

At its worst, looking at social media at the wrong times can cause irreversible damage. People have lost their jobs because of checking social media too often while at work. Others have sustained serious injuries or even died because they were focused on social media when they should have been paying attention to their immediate surroundings. Again, it seems obvious, but we should always put our and other people's safety ahead of our need to check social media.

Cyberbullying

Cyberbullying is when bullies use digital tools like text messages, email, and social media to harass their victims. It can involve text bombing, cruel tweets or

Facebook posts, posting humiliating photos of the victim, impersonating the victim, disclosing (true or false) personal information about the victim to a wide audience online, and much more. With each new social media platform that launches, there are new ways for bullies to abuse innocent people.

Cyberbullying is particularly dangerous because, unlike regular bullying, it can happen at any time or place, and it can be hard to trace the perpetrators. Before social media, victims of bullying could generally find safe spaces where their bullies couldn't reach them (their homes, places with a lot of witnesses), but now bullies' reach extends everywhere there is Wi-Fi or cellphone reception.

The only way to 100 percent ensure that you won't be affected by cyberbullying is to never sign in to social media. Even blocking the bullies' accounts is not a permanent fix, because they can always create new accounts under false names that you won't recognize. One way to minimize cyberbullying is to make sure you only add people who you already know and feel safe interacting with. Another way to combat cyberbullying is to create your own social media accounts under a false name that only your friends and family know. This way the bullies shouldn't be able to find you online. If you ever are

(continued on the next page)

One of the most dangerous things about cyberbullying is its invisibility. If someone is sending you cruel messages, don't keep it to yourself.

(continued from the previous page)

on the receiving end of cyberbullying, make sure you screenshot it so that you have evidence if he or she deletes the cruel material. Just like all bullying, it's important to tell someone if you're experiencing cyberbullying. It's much easier to handle if you have support than trying to do so on your own.

Although most social media anxiety involves wanting to check social media, victims of cyberbullying often feel anxious about using social media, afraid they will be exposing themselves to more abuse.

Avoiding Social Media

Most of the time social media anxiety is characterized by feeling anxious while unable to check social media, but in some cases the reverse can be true. Some people with social media anxiety feel anxious *about* checking social media. They worry that someone will have unfriended them, that there will be bad news waiting from their family back home, or even just that they'll get caught up in social media and end up spending too much time online, and so they avoid signing in to their accounts even when they have important reasons to do so. Although these people may not spend as much time on social media as others with social media anxiety, they still spend an unhealthy amount of time thinking about it, which is just as harmful.

Avoiding social media can lead to people isolating themselves. For many people, social media is their main way of keeping in touch with friends and family, and their main way of sharing what is happening in their lives. Unless they make a concerted effort to keep up to date with the people in their lives via other means, people who avoid social media can easily fall out of touch and lose important relationships. Not going on social media also deprives them of the ability to share what is happening in their own lives, meaning they might receive less support if they're going through a hard time, simply because no one else knows about it.

This is not only a social issue. People who avoid using social media can miss out on significant opportunities because they aren't putting themselves in the right position to grasp them. A lot of jobs are now advertised on social media, either directly by the companies or by their staff

More and more jobs are being advertised over social media. If you don't have an account, you could be missing out on career opportunities.

sharing the vacancies on their personal accounts. It's common for people to get a job at a company because they already know someone who works there, but if you don't see your friend's post about an open position, then knowing her isn't going to help you. The same is true for housing. A person will often share on social media if he or she is looking for someone to share an apartment with, if he or she is subletting his or her room while out of town, or if he or she is selling his or her house. Many people would prefer to live with, or pass their home on to, someone they already know and trust, but of course you have to know this is happening in order to take advantage of it. Other times, using social media can help make the most of an opportunity you already have. If your band is playing a gig and you don't make a Facebook event inviting people to it, there

The next time you're hanging out with friends, pause and look around. How many of you are more focused on your devices than the people around you?

is a much lower chance of people finding out about it and attending.

Some people avoid social media in this way because they have used it too much in the past and suffered from the negative effects of social media overuse. While many people do just fine without social media in their lives, if avoiding social media is causing issues in your life, then you're just trading one set of problems for another. The important thing is to make sure that you have a healthy relationship with social media, no matter how much you use it.

Changing Your Relationship with Social Media

The most effective way to beat social media anxiety is to change your relationship with social media. This can mean cutting back on how often you sign in to your accounts or just changing the time of day you look at social media. Sometimes changing your relationship with social media doesn't mean changing how you use social media at all but instead changing the way you think about social media.

Before you can change your relationship with social media you need to identify how you use social media. Do you check Tumblr first thing every morning? Do you flick between different social media platforms while eating lunch? Do you stay up late keeping up with Pinterest? Often people find themselves scrolling through social media without ever having planned to sign in. In order to change these behaviors, you first need to recognize your patterns and habits.

How Much

The average person uses social media for almost two hours a day, according to Global Web Index. It's even more for teenagers, with some sources claiming thirteen- to eighteen-year-olds spend up to nine hours a day on social media. Keep in mind that these are averages; some people don't use social media at all, and others are using it even more than these figures suggest. If you're struggling with social media anxiety, it may be because you are spending too much time on social media and becoming dependent on it. Try recording how much time you spend on social media in one day. All those quick glances at Twitter on your tablet add up. You might be surprised by how much of your day is taken up scrolling through your feeds.

If you're unhappy with the amount of time you're spending on social media or you think it's contributing to your social media anxiety, it's time to try cutting back. The most effective way to cut down the amount of time you spend on social media each day is to set a strict limit—say one hour, for example. You can

It can be difficult, but many people find that limiting the amount of time they spend on social media increases their quality of life.

allocate this time in any way you choose: half an hour in the morning then another half hour in the evening, twelve five-minute bursts throughout the day, or one long session. The only rule is once your time is up, it's up. No more social media until tomorrow.

If you're finding this too difficult, you may be trying too much all at once. It can be very difficult to break habits and change routines. Perhaps try setting a higher, more achievable limit. Once you've had some success holding yourself to four hours of social media a day, you can move down to three and a half, three, then two and a half until you reach a point where you feel good about the amount of time you're spending on social media. Once you've achieved this, all you have to do is maintain it.

Don't get too down on yourself if you do occasionally slip up and go over your social media limit. Change takes time and not every day is the same. If something especially important or exciting happens one day, maybe it's OK to spend longer than usual on social media talking to people about it. Spending a few extra hours on social media once in a while isn't going to do you any harm. The important thing here is habits: if you find yourself overusing social media on a more regular basis, it may be time to start thinking of other ways to control your usage. But tomorrow is always a new start. Just because you spent five hours on social media today doesn't mean you can't go back to one hour tomorrow.

Changes in How We Use the Internet

Since the World Wide Web was released to the public on April 30, 1993, the ways people use the internet have changed drastically. In that first year there were fourteen million internet users in the world and only 130 websites. Now there are more than three billion internet users and more than one billion websites, and the numbers just keep going up.

At first the internet was mainly used by researchers and academics at universities, but as the web became more accessible, more and more of the general public began to get online. In those early days the internet was mostly used as a source of information and was mainly made up of text. Amazon, which launched in 1995, was the first major commercial website, but back then it only sold books, a far cry from its current list of departments, selling everything from food to clothes to motorcycles.

As connections improved and speeds increased, people were able to use the internet for different

(continued on the next page)

(continued from the previous page)

things. They went from reading the internet to looking at pictures, playing games, downloading music, streaming music, and watching videos online. Now many people don't even have televisions, choosing

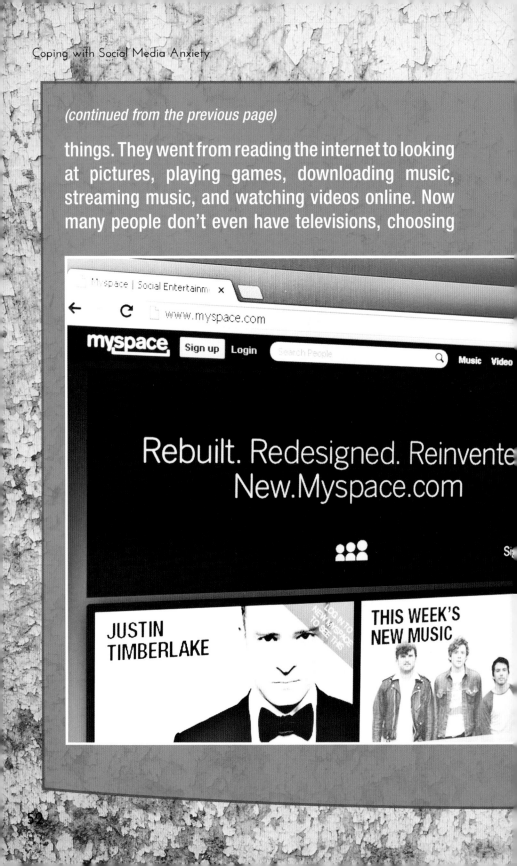

instead to stream their favorite shows online through websites like Netflix or Hulu.

SixDegrees, the first social medial site, rolled out in 1997 and lasted until 2001, but it wasn't until Myspace came around in 2003 that social media really took off. It paved the way for platforms like Facebook, Twitter, Tumblr, Instagram, and more. As of June 8, 2016, people spend an average of 30 percent of their time online on social media, according to Global Web Index.

With the proliferation of smartphones, now people are using the internet without even having to access websites; instead they are using apps like Uber, Spotify, and Facetime to get directions, play games, do their banking, and much more.

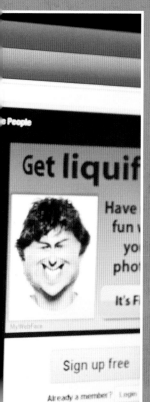

MySpace was relaunched by Justin Timberlake in 2013, but the new platform didn't take off, and it never regained its earlier popularity.

When

Everyone has different social media habits. Many people check Facebook first thing when they wake up in the morning. Others stay on Tumblr late into the night. Some people only look at social media while on the bus to and from school. Sometimes people experience social media anxiety not because of how much time they spend on social media but *when* they use social media. If you're a morning social media user, you might find yourself always running late to school, which causes stress. Nighttime social media users are more likely to have trouble sleeping, which tends to lead to being in a bad mood the next day.

If you're struggling to cope with social media anxiety, try to figure out which times of day you use social media the most. Could that be contributing to your problems? What if you tried changing the time of day you use social media? Experiment with it. One day you could try only using social media after school; the next you could just use it until lunchtime and then stop. There's no set rule about when is the healthiest time of the day to use social media; it's different for everyone. You may even find that certain platforms work better for you at certain times of the day. Maybe checking Facebook in the morning causes you anxiety, but looking at Snapchat when you wake up works as a great start to your day.

Find it easy to get caught up in social media? Always running late? Try only checking your accounts in the evenings once you've fulfilled all your obligations.

The one thing to steer away from is using social media right before bed because of the effect it can have on your sleep, but even this doesn't affect everyone. Some people sleep just fine after looking at Instagram for a few hours. It's all about figuring out your relationship with social media. After some experimenting, hopefully you'll be able to find certain times of day (or even days of the week) when using social media doesn't have such a negative effect on your mental well-being. Try to confine your social media use to those times: it could have a huge effect on your anxiety levels. If you can't find a time of day when social media works better for you, never fear, there are other aspects of your relationship with it that you can control.

Where

Much like *when* you use social media, *where* you use social media can have an impact on whether it causes you anxiety. Often, where you use social media is related to what else you are doing, or meant to be doing, while you're spending time networking. If you spend a lot of time on LinkedIn at work, then you're probably not getting much of your actual work done, which can lead to you worrying about deadlines and fear of being caught while off task. As a way of dealing

Not only does staying off social media during meals help you connect with the people around you, but you're also less likely to spill food on yourself.

with that stress and further avoiding your work, you may end up spending even more time on LinkedIn, creating a cycle of social media anxiety.

One way to combat social media anxiety is to set up social-media-free zones, places where you're not allowed to use social media. If you often find yourself checking Facebook during dinner while the rest of your family is talking about their days, that might have a negative effect on your relationship with them, so you might want to consider banning yourself from social media at the dinner table. Other places to consider making off-limits are school, work, your bedroom, and social events. These are the places where social media is most likely to have a negative effect on your well-being, but, of course, it's different for everyone: sometimes there's nothing better than sending a few Snapchats from a party. You need to figure out where social media works for you.

You could even consider making your phone or tablet itself a social-media-free zone by deleting all of your social media apps. This would mean you could only use social media when actually in front of a computer, which would significantly decrease the amount of multitasking involved. It would also serve to further limit *when* you could use social media. You can't just pull your laptop out of your pocket to check Google+ while you're waiting for the streetlight to change color. It may take some time to get used to, but this type of controlled environment can be extremely useful for combating anxiety. Once you get accustomed to only using social media in certain places at certain times, you will learn not to spend energy worrying about it the rest of the time, leading to a much healthier relationship and less anxiety.

How Many

Another part of your relationship with social media to consider is how many and which different platforms you're using. Maybe the reason you're spending too much time online is because you're trying to keep up with more platforms than you can manage. Perhaps you only find one or two of those platforms satisfying and the others are just adding stress to your life. If that's the case, it's probably time to cut down on the number of different social media platforms you're using.

Every social media platform has a different focus and design. They all have their pros and cons. Instagram is based around photos. Snapchat is all about brief videos. Twitter is predominantly text. Facebook has a little bit of everything. If your social media anxiety stems from not wanting to miss out on events your friends are attending, then you might want to stick with Facebook and delete a couple of your other accounts. If your problem is that you're constantly sending Snapchats, then perhaps you should delete Snapchat from your device and try just using other social media platforms for a while.

According to Global Web Index, the average person has accounts on more than five different social media platforms. That's a lot to keep up with, and most people don't. The same report shows that

Sometimes cutting out just one social media platform is all you need to do to make things feel more manageable.

most people are only actively using 2.8 different social media platforms. That's a much more reasonable figure. If you're feeling overwhelmed by how much is happening on social media that you need to stay up to date with, you are probably using too many different platforms. Try to figure out which ones you get the most out of, keep those accounts, and delete the rest. There's no point in having an account on a social media platform if all it's doing is causing you anxiety.

Another thing to consider is how many people you are connected with on each platform. According to researchers from Oxford University, the average Facebook user has 155 friends but would only trust four of them in an emergency. Professor Robin Dunbar has found that the human brain cannot maintain relationships with many more than 150 people, a figure very close to the average number of Facebook friends. So perhaps if you're finding social media overwhelming, it's not because you're using too many platforms but because you're connected with too many people on the platforms you do use. If you have a lot of friends on a particular social network, perhaps you should try unfollowing some of them and see how it affects your mental state.

Tools

Social media is a tool that people use to keep in touch with friends and family, connect with new people who share similar interests, share their creative work, and record significant memories. All of this is positive and should be encouraged. It's when we become too dependent on it that the tool of social media stops being a benefit and starts causing us problems. But there are some other tools that can help us control our relationship with social media so that we can enjoy the benefits without the negative effects.

One thing that can really help is investing in an alarm clock. Sure, your phone probably has a built-in alarm function and using that might be more convenient, but it can also make it harder to avoid social media. If the first thing you do when you wake up is pick up your phone to turn the alarm off, it can

There's nothing like a good old-fashioned alarm clock to get you up and out of bed in the morning.

be tempting to check social media right away instead of getting up and getting ready for the day. Having an alarm clock also means that you don't have to keep your phone within arm's reach all night long (you could even keep it in another room!), so you won't be disturbed by notifications during the night.

There is a whole range of apps out there specifically designed to help you track and control how much time you spend on social media. Apps like Offtime and Breakfree have a whole host of functions, like providing analysis of how you use your phone, monitoring your goals of how much you want to use your phone, blocking the use of certain apps for certain periods of time, auto-rejecting phone calls—the list goes on and on. If you're struggling to manage your social media use on your own, these apps can be very useful. Trying to maintain a low "addiction score" can even become a kind of game.

Your phone itself probably has a few features that can help you manage your social media use. All smartphones have a built-in option called Flight Mode, which prevents your phone from sending or receiving signals. If you need to get some homework done without distractions, it might help to put your phone on airplane mode. Many phones also have other means of limiting their use, often designed to prevent children from accessing inappropriate content but usually just as useful for controlling your social media use. For example, iPhones have a section in their settings called Restrictions, which allows you to block your phone from using specific apps or visiting particular websites. And there's always the last resort: the trusty power button. Sometimes the best solution is the simplest, and it makes the most sense just to turn your phone off.

CHAPTER FOUR

Unplugging

If you've tried to change your relationship with social media but nothing seems to work, it might be time to trying unplugging and taking a break from all social media for a while. Some people are just incompatible with social media; no matter what they do or how they use it, they end up worse off than they would be without it. For other people, unplugging is just a temporary thing that gives them time and space to reset, and then they can return to social media with a new perspective and a healthier relationship to it. No matter what your reason for unplugging, there are certain ways you can prepare for it to make your experience more successful.

Set a Time Period

Once you've decided to unplug, the next decision you need to make is how long you're committing to do it for. If you don't set an end date for your

Most people never turn off their phones, not even at the movies, but if social media is making you anxious, the best option might be to switch your phone off completely.

social media fasting, you are much more likely to give up early. There's no right or wrong length of time to give up social media. If you just want to see what it's like and what your immediate reaction to it is, you could just sign out for twenty-four hours. Or, if you're committed to making a significant change to your lifestyle, you could decide to unplug for a whole year.

For whatever period of time you decide to unplug, it's important to make sure that your goal is realistic and that you are prepared for everything it entails. It's probably not a good idea to decide today that you want to unplug for a year and then go ahead and deactivate all your accounts right away. You need to take some time to think about this. You don't want to unplug two weeks before your birthday and lose out on an easy way to organize your party.

If you're planning to unplug for an extended period of time, you will want to check that you have other ways to get in touch with the important people in your life. You don't want to delete all your social media accounts and then realize that you have no way of contacting your best friend. Because there can be unexpected consequences to unplugging from social media, it is recommended that you start by unplugging for a short time first, say a week, and then building up to longer periods without social media. After all, if you reach the end of the time you had planned to unplug for and you want to keep going, there's no reason why you can't. Just set a new date you want to be social media-free until and see how you feel once you reach it.

Let People Know

Before you lock yourself out of social media, make sure you have let people know what's about to happen. If you suddenly stop posting online, with no warning or obvious reason, the people who interact with you on social media might worry about you. They would have no way of knowing that this was something you had planned to do and could think that you're unwell or in danger.

It's a good idea to make a post on each of your social media accounts well in advance of unplugging (at least a couple of days before) to let everyone know that you won't be on social media for the foreseeable future. You can also use this post to give people alternate ways of getting in contact with you, such as by email or text. If you don't want to make this information accessible to all the people with whom you're connected, you could write something such as "private message me for my email address" and only respond to people who you want to stay in touch with. If you're making this post on Facebook you can actually set which of your friends will be able to see it, avoiding some awkward situations.

The reason it's important to make these kinds of posts in advance of unplugging is that you want to give people a chance to actually see them. If you make a post and then immediately delete your account, not many people are going to see it and there won't have been much point in making it at all. Also, if you're asking your friends to message you to get your contact information, you need to give them time to do that. If you don't make the effort to inform your friends about what you're doing and ensure that you can contact them and they can contact you, then you run the risk of isolating yourself, which could make unplugging a negative experience.

Lock Yourself Out

The next step is to lock yourself out of social media. Just signing out of your accounts isn't enough. You want to make it as difficult as possible for you to access your accounts, so you'll be less tempted to give up on your

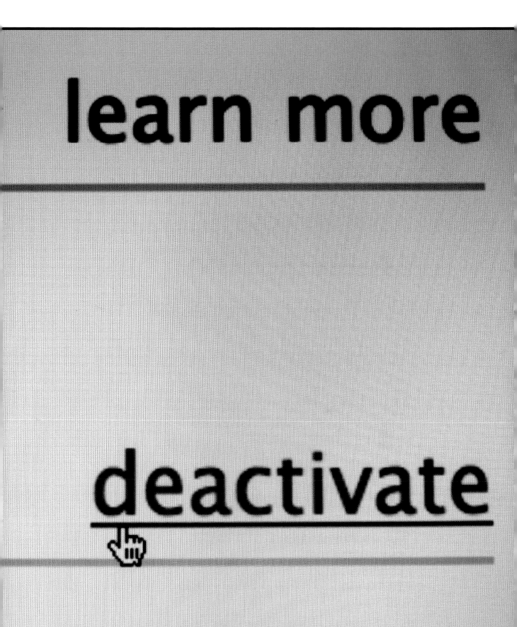

Deactivating your account isn't permanent; you can always reactivate it later, once you have a more healthy relationship with social media.

goal. You don't want it to be easy to sign back in and check social media without even thinking about it.

There are various ways of locking yourself out of your social media accounts. Some social media platforms make a distinction between deleting and deactivating your account. For instance, if you deactivate your Facebook account all of your information is retained on the website but it can't be accessed by anyone unless you reactivate your account. Whereas if you delete your account, all of your information is lost forever, and it is impossible to get your account back. Both options have their pros and cons. If you deactivate your account, it's much easier to transition back into using Facebook once you've finished your time without social media, but reactivating your account only requires you to sign back in to your account, so it's much easier to give into the temptation and return to Facebook. If you delete your account, however, there's no temptation to sign back in, because it's impossible. The downside is that when you decide to go back to using social media, you'll have to create a whole new account from scratch. If you decide to delete your accounts, make sure you save any information you don't want to lose. If Instagram is the only place you have your photos archived, you might want to download them onto your computer before deleting your account.

PASSWORD

* *

If you don't know your password, you can't overuse social media because you won't be able to log in to your account—it's as simple as that.

Another option is to change the passwords on your social media accounts to something that you don't know and then logging out so that you won't be able to sign

Internet Addiction

Social media isn't the only thing people get addicted to online. Even before social media became such a huge part of our daily lives, people were overusing the internet for gaming, gambling, shopping, and pornography. These types of addictions can have even worse consequences than social media. People have gone into massive debt from addiction to online gambling and shopping. Parents in China and South Korea are so concerned about their children's addiction to the internet (particularly gaming) that they send them to boot camps to detox. Addiction to online gaming is one of the most widespread and dangerous forms of internet addiction, to the point where some psychologists consider it a clinical condition. Some people's addictions have been so severe that they play online computer games nonstop until they die.

back in. If you choose this option, you need to make sure you'll be able to access your password once you're ready to return to social media. There are a few ways to do this: you could write the password down somewhere you're sure it won't get lost, you could get a friend to change the password for you, or you could just make sure that you know the answers to your security questions so you can use the "forgot your password" function. You've just got to make sure you don't give up and access your password before you've reached your goal.

Once you've locked yourself out, it's time to delete all the social media apps off your phone and/or tablet and block the websites on your computer. This will help by removing the constant reminders that you're avoiding social media and lessen the temptation to give up and sign back in.

Don't Isolate Yourself

It's important to make sure you don't isolate yourself during your time away from social media. It's increasingly common, especially among those with social media anxiety, for people to get the majority of their social interaction through social media. While you're unplugged, the key is to replace those interactions with other forms of communication. This is why you must make sure you have your friends' and family's contact details before you lock yourself out of social media.

There are plenty of ways to maintain a social life without using social media. People did it for thousands of years, after all. You can call or text people, write letters or postcards, organize regular hangouts, meet for lunch or go to a movie together, or plan trips with people. The positive side of all of these types of social activities is that they encourage more in-depth communication with people than you usually get from social media. During these interactions you'll be spending much longer time with people than you do when you quickly scan their status updates online. This extended and more focused time spent with people leads to more meaningful relationships with them.

In addition to making sure you stay connected to your friends and family, time off of social media can also serve as an opportunity to connect with new people. There are probably people you spend time with regularly who you've never spoken to: regulars on your bus, at the place

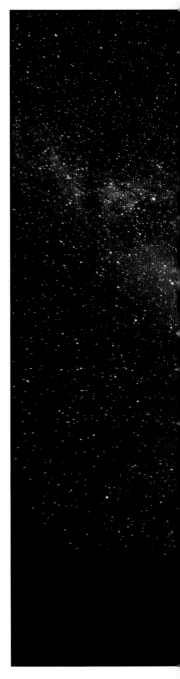

Yes, there's a lot of interesting stuff online, but there's a whole universe outside of social media to explore as well.

you usually eat lunch, and the people who work at your local library. What if, instead of spending the time you're around these people absorbed in your phone, you struck up a conversation with one of them? You have at least one thing in common; maybe they could be friendships just waiting to happen.

Find Substitutes

It's not just social interactions that you will need to replace while you're off of social media. A lot of the time people spend on social media is not directly used to interact with their friends: much of it is spent aimlessly scrolling, checking to see if anything new has been posted even though they just looked two minutes ago, or clicking on links and reading articles that they never would have spent their time on if someone they knew hadn't shared it on social media.

It's important to find compelling things to fill the time you used to occupy with social media, because otherwise that time will be spent obsessing over the fact that you're not on social media, which isn't much of an improvement. This is a good chance to do some of the things you've always wanted to do but never had the time or discipline to follow through with: start exercising more, take an art class, or finally learn to knit. What kinds of activities you choose to use your new free time for can depend on how and when you used to

Activities that keep your hands occupied are especially useful because they stop your hands from drifting toward your phone out of habit.

use social media. If you always spent an hour first thing in the morning catching up on all your different feeds, then maybe you could use that time to go for a run or have a proper breakfast for once. Whereas, if you were a late-night Pinterest scroller, that time might be better spent reading a book or maybe even just getting to sleep earlier.

Another thing to consider is that many people habitually pull out their phones to check social media without even thinking about it or while they are waiting for something. It's useful to find something else to occupy yourself with in these situations, preferably something that involves using your hands, so it fills the same role as pulling out your phone. Perhaps try carrying a sketchpad with you to doodle on or a Rubik's Cube or some other kind of puzzle.

CHAPTER FIVE

Asking for Help

Coping with social media anxiety isn't easy, and sometimes no matter how hard you try, it's something that you can't do alone. Different people will be able to help you with different things, so don't feel embarrassed to reach out to a few people you're close to and ask for some support. The chances are that they'll be happy to help you in whatever way they can.

Friends and Family

Your friends and family should be the first people you turn to when dealing with something difficult like social media anxiety. They care about you and your well-being, so they are invested in finding solutions to your problems because what affects you affects them. Not only that but they are also some of the people with whom you spend the most time in your day-to-day life and so are well situated to help you change your habits.

If you live far away from your family or you don't have a good relationship with them, don't worry: your friends will be happy to support you; that's what they're there for. If you feel confident enough, you can also ask your classmates or the people you work with to help you in place of family or friends because you spend a lot of time around them as well, and you're probably friendly with at least some of them.

Interacting Offline

One of the best ways for your friends and family to help you cope with social media anxiety is to spend time with you in person. Instead of keeping in touch with you online, they could invite you over for a meal or you could go out and do something together. Not only will this mean you won't have to turn to social media to interact with them but if they can engage you enough, you won't feel compelled to check what's happening online while you're with them. You can even do things together where it is impossible to use social media, like swimming or rock climbing. The more time you spend with people in person, the less time you'll have to spend online, and the less reason you'll have to go on social media.

Get out and do something physical. You can't just casually check Twitter when your hands are busy holding you up high above the ground.

Holding You Accountable

Your friends and family can be helpful another way by holding you accountable for your social media use. If you tell them that you're trying to cut back on your social media use or even quitting completely, they can call you out if they see you commenting on a post or checking your phone while you're with them. This takes some of the pressure off of you, so you don't always have to be self-disciplined and resist temptation. If no one else knows you're trying not to use social media, then it's completely up to you to make sure you're not using it. If your friends and family know, however, then you have some backup just in case you ever slip up.

Changing Your Passwords

Your friends or family can even go a step farther toward helping you stay off social media by locking you out themselves. If they can see that you can't help yourself from logging back in to your accounts and checking them, no matter what you or they have done to try and prevent it, they can offer to change your passwords to something that you won't be able to guess. By doing this they are taking the responsibility for your social media use away from you and putting it on their own shoulders. If you come to them begging to be let back onto your Google+ account, telling them it's an emergency, it will be up to them to decide whether to give you access. This can be a lot of pressure, so if someone does it for you, try not to make it too hard on him or her. You don't want to take advantage of your friends.

Professional Help

The other people you can ask for help with your social media anxiety are the professionals: doctors, counselors, therapists, and psychologists. These people are qualified to be able to deal with the situations you're experiencing. They've seen these problems before, and it's their job to handle them in the most appropriate way. If they don't know how to help you, then they will know who can and refer you to him or her.

If social media is the only thing causing you anxiety, then you probably won't need sustained professional help, but checking in with your doctor can't hurt. If social media anxiety is only a part of a bigger problem for you, however, then therapy might be just what you need.

General Practitioner

The first step to take if you're considering consulting a mental health professional is to consult with your general practitioner (GP). This is your regular doctor who you go to when you have a virus or when you need to get some shots before traveling. Hopefully you've known him or her for a while and have a good relationship, where you feel comfortable talking to him or her about what you're experiencing.

Your GP can assess your symptoms and determine whether you are suffering from a mental health condition. Once you've spoken to your doctor, he or she will help you to decide what the best course of action is. If your GP thinks therapy is a good option, he or she can refer you to a variety of specialists in your area. If your GP thinks medication might help, he or she can prescribe you something. Or, if neither of those options is right for you, your GP might suggest something else, like having you come in for more regular checkups to keep an eye on the situation.

If you don't have a general practitioner with whom you have a good relationship, an alternative first stop is your school counselor. Although your counselor can't prescribe medication, he or she should be able to offer all the same services as a general practitioner, and the counselor is likely

It's tempting to self-diagnose with all the information available on the internet, but not all of it is reliable. Only a qualified medical professional can give you a trustworthy diagnosis.

more experienced in dealing with these specific issues, especially in people your age.

Cognitive Behavioral Therapy

If your GP or school counselor refers you to a therapist, he or she will most likely be practicing a form of cognitive behavioral therapy (CBT). CBT is the most widely used form of therapy for treating mental disorders, including anxiety and depression. The focus of CBT is to change how you think. The theory is that changing your thoughts will change your behaviors, which will in turn change your feelings. For instance, if social media is making you feel anxious because you feel overwhelmed trying to keep up with everything that your friends are posting, you might be thinking, "I need to stay up to date with everything on Facebook." Your therapist would then help you to instead think, "It doesn't matter if I miss something on social media occasionally." This would lead you to check social media less often and feel less anxious and overwhelmed by it.

Other Forms Of Therapy

Although cognitive behavioral therapy is the most common treatment for anxiety and other similar mental disorders, it doesn't work for everyone and there are alternatives. In fact, there are far too many varieties of therapy to list here, so we will just go over a few that can be useful for dealing with anxiety.

Exposure therapy is specifically designed to treat anxiety disorders. It basically does what the name says: it exposes patients to the things that cause them distress. The idea is that the more often you are exposed to the object or situation, the more accustomed to it you will become, the more in control you will feel, and the less anxiety you will experience. Exposure therapy uses a technique called systematic desensitization, in which you take small steps to build up your confidence before facing the thing that you're afraid of. For example, if you're anxious about using social media because you have experienced cyberbullying in the past, you might begin by just looking at screenshots from various social media platforms, then imagining using them, then just signing in and looking at other people's pages for a few minutes, and eventually posting something on your own page.

Occupational therapy is another form of therapy that is often used to treat anxiety and is often viewed as especially useful for younger patients. The goal of occupational therapy is to help the patient acquire or regain the skills needed for daily life. It is less focused on thoughts than on concrete actions people can take to deal with their problems and to prevent problems from occurring in the first place. Some of the skills on which an occupational therapist might focus with someone experiencing social media anxiety are time management, breathing techniques, developing

Sometimes therapy makes you feel worse in the moment because it brings up thoughts and emotions that you usually try to close off.

healthy sleep patterns, and conversational skills. These skills will help the person be less dependent on social media and deal better with it when he or she is using it.

It's important to note that therapists will often use a combination of different forms of therapy in treating a single patient. Each person is unique and will respond differently to different techniques. A therapist's job is to find the most effective way of treating each individual patient, whether that be straight-ahead cognitive behavioral therapy or elements of both occupational therapy and exposure therapy, or other techniques like hypnotherapy or art therapy.

Also remember that therapists aren't one size fits all. Not every therapist works well for everyone. No matter what their qualifications, they're still just people, and some people don't get along. If you're not getting along with your therapist, it's OK to ask to see someone else; he or she will understand. It has happened to the therapist before and it will happen again. Just because it's not working with you and one particular therapist doesn't mean that therapy can't be helpful for you—you probably just haven't found the right person yet.

No matter how your social media anxiety presents itself, be it constantly checking Instagram to see if your latest photo has received any more likes or avoiding Facebook altogether because it's too much to handle, there's something you can do about it. You can deal with it on your own if that's what's most comfortable for you, or you can also ask someone else for help. Whatever you do, make sure you start now. It's easy to put off dealing with your problems, but the only way to cope with social media anxiety is to take action to change your situation.

10 Great Questions to Ask a Psychologist

1. Do you think social media anxiety should be classified as a clinical condition?

2. How is social media anxiety different from social anxiety disorder?

3. Am I suffering solely from social media anxiety or am I also experiencing other mental disorders?

4. Is medication an effective way to treat social media anxiety?

5. Should I unplug from social media entirely or just cut back on how much I use it?

6. What do you think the best form of therapy would be for my situation?

7. Have you seen an increase in the number of people experiencing social media anxiety?

8. Which social media platforms have you found cause the most people anxiety?

9. How is anxiety caused by social media different from anxiety caused by other things?

10. On the whole, do you think social media is more of a help or a hindrance to people?

Glossary

account A social media user's profile, which allows him or her to access the platform by signing in with his or her username and password and stores all his or her information.

anxiety A feeling of worry, stress, or inner turmoil about a future event.

anxiety disorders Mental health conditions characterized by feeling unhealthy levels of anxiety.

apps Applications, especially programs that can be downloaded onto mobile devices. They have many uses, including communication, gaming, and navigation.

blue light The light given off by screens that signals to the brain that it is time to wake up.

cognitive behavioral therapy (CBT) A form of therapy that focuses on changing people's thoughts and behaviors.

cyberbullying When people use social media and other forms of digital communication to bully others.

deactivate Temporarily closing a social media account, thereby making it inaccessible, but saving the information so the account can be reopened.

delete Permanently removing an account from a social media platform and getting rid of all the information stored on it.

fear of missing out (FOMO) When people feel anxious or do something they don't feel like doing just because they don't want to miss anything.

feed The main page of a social media platform where all the posts by people with whom a user is connected appear.

multitasking When people try to do two or more things at once but actually just switch quickly back and forth between them.

notification A message that pops up on a mobile device, usually sent by an app to inform the user of something that has happened.

platforms Different social media services, such as Facebook, Twitter, and Instagram.

post When a user shares text, images, audio, video, or anything else from his or her computer or device on a social media platform.

scrolling Moving up and down through social media feeds to navigate through content that has been posted.

selfie A photo someone takes of himself or herself, usually with a cell phone.

smartphone A mobile phone with functions similar to a computer, with the ability to run apps and access the internet.

social media Websites and apps people use to connect with people, communicate, and share content.

unplugging When people remove themselves from social media for an extended period of time.

Anxiety and Depression Association of America
8701 Georgia Avenue, Suite 412
Silver Spring, MD 20910
(240) 485-1035
Email: information@adaa.org
Website: www.adaa.org
Facebook: @
AnxietyAndDepressionAssociationOfAmerica
Twitter: @Got_Anxiety
Pinterest: Anxiety and Depression Association of
America

The Anxiety and Depression Association of
America is focused on improving life for people
who experience anxiety, depressive, and other
disorders. It does this through education,
support, and resources, as well as by helping
people find treatment.

AnxietyBC
311-409 Granville Street
Vancouver, BC V6C 1T2
Canada
(604) 620-0744
Website: www.anxietybc.com
Facebook: @AnxietyBC

Twitter: @AnxietyBC

YouTube: AnxietyBC

AnxietyBC is an organization committed to educating people about anxiety. It developed a smartphone app called MindShift to help people take charge of their anxiety.

Anxiety.org

4600 Campus Drive, Suite 107

Newport Beach, CA 92660

(949) 267-4117

Website: https://www.anxiety.org/anxiety-disorder-social-media

Facebook: @AnxietyDotOrg

Twitter: @Anxietyorg

Instagram: @anxietydotorg

Pinterest: @anxietyorg

The Anxiety.org website partners with schools, researchers, therapists, and other mental health and wellness experts, just to name a few, to provide accessible resources that may help people recover from all varieties of anxiety, including social media anxiety disorders.

The Cybersmile Foundation

530 Lytton Avenue, 2nd Floor

Palo Alto, CA 94301

(650) 617-3474

Email: help@cybersmile.org

Website: www.cybersmile.org

Facebook: @TheCybersmileFoundation

Twitter: @CybersmileHQ

Instagram: @cybersmilefoundation

The Cybersmile Foundation is a nonprofit organization dedicated to combating cyberbullying and digital abuse. It has trained advisers available 24/7 for support and education.

reSTART

1001 290th Avenue SE

Fall City, WA 98024

(800) 682-6934

Email: connect@restartlife.com

Website: www.netaddictionrecovery.com

Facebook: @netaddictionrecovery

Twitter: @ReStartYourLife

YouTube: reSTART Life

reStart is a treatment center for people addicted to digital media. It offers a range of different programs including retreats, family coaching, and counseling.

Teen Line

Cedars-Sinai

PO Box 48750

Los Angeles, CA 90048-0750

(800) 852-8336

Email: admin@teenlineonline.org

Website: www.teenline.org

Facebook: @teenlineonline

Twitter: @teenlineonline

Tumblr: teenlineonline

Teen Line is a helpline for teenagers where the people listening to you and giving you advice are also teenagers. They are ready to help with any problems, including those that involve anxiety and social media.

Turning Point Youth Services

95 Wellesley Street East

Toronto, ON M4Y 2X9

Canada

(416) 925-9250

Website: www.turningpoint.ca

Facebook: @TurningPointYouthServices

Turning Point Youth Services offers counseling,
residential care, and treatment to people between
the ages of twelve and twenty-four. Its expertise
is in dealing with issues that young people face,
such as anxiety, bullying, and issues at school.

Websites

Because of the changing nature of internet links,
Rosen Publishing has developed an online list of
websites related to the subject of this book. This site
is updated regularly. Please use this link to access
this list:

http://www.rosenlinks.com/COP/Media

For Further Reading

Boyd, Danah. *It's Complicated: The Social Lives of Networked Teens.* New Haven, CT: Yale University Press, 2015.

Bradley, Michael J. *Crazy-Stressed.* New York, NY: AMACOM, 2017.

Larson, Paul. *Safe & Sound: Social Media.* Huntington Beach, CA: Teacher Created Materials, 2017.

Maushart, Susan. *The Winter of Our Disconnect.* New York, NY: TarcherPerigee, 2011.

Ockler, Sarah. *#scandal.* New York, NY: Simon Pulse, 2014.

Perdew, Laura. *Internet Addiction.* Minneapolis, MN: Essential Library, 2014.

Peterson, Lois. *Disconnect.* Victoria, BC, Canada: Orca Currents, 2012.

Porterfield, Jason. *Teen Stress and Anxiety* (Teen Mental Health). New York, NY: Rosen Publishing, 2014.

Sales, Nancy Jo. *American Girls: Social Media and the Secret Lives of Teenagers.* New York, NY: Vintage, 2017.

Shannon, Jennifer. *The Anxiety Survival Guide for Teens.* Oakland, CA: Instant Help, 2015.

Staley, Erin. *Defeating Stress and Anxiety* (Effective Survival Strategies). New York, NY: Rosen Publishing, 2016.

Vejby, Rune. *Text in Sick: How Smartphones, Texting, and Social Media Are Changing Our Relationships.* Los Angeles, CA: Gravitate Research Group, 2015.

Bibliography

Almaatouq, Abdullah, Laura Radaelli, Alex Pentland, and Erez Shmueli. "Are You Your Friends' Friend? Poor Perception of Friendship Ties Limits the Ability to Promote Behavioral Change." *PLoS ONE* 11, no. 3 (March 22, 2016). http://journals.plos.org/plosone/article?id=10.1371/journal.pone.0151588.

AOTA. "Occupational Therapy's Role in Mental Health Promotion, Prevention, & Intervention With Children & Youth—Anxiety Disorders." Retrieved March 4, 2017. http://www.aota.org/-/media/corporate/files/practice/children/schoolmhtoolkit/anxiety%20disorders%20info%20sheet.pdf.

Bennett, Megan. "Social Media Linked to Student Anxiety." *Columbia Chronicle* (May 12, 2014). http://www.columbiachronicle.com/health_and_tech/article_aa2daa9a-d7e4-11e3-9286-001a4bcf6878.html.

British Psychological Society. "Pressure to Be Available 24/7 on Social Media Causes Teen Anxiety, Depression." Science Daily, September 11, 2015. https://www.sciencedaily.com/releases/2015/09/150911094917.htm.

Buchanan, Erin. "Occupational Therapy and Anxiety." *OT Magazine* (Jan/Feb 2017).

Buckle, Chase. "2 Hours Per Day Spent on Social Media & Messaging." Global Web Index, July

25, 2016. https://www.globalwebindex.net/blog/2-hours-per-day-spent-on-social-media-messaging.

Common Sense Media. "Common Sense Census: Media Use by Tweens and Teens." March 2015. https://www.commonsensemedia.org/research/the-common-sense-census-media-use-by-tweens-and-teens.

Davey, Graham C. L. "Social Media, Loneliness, and Anxiety in Young People." *Psychology Today* (December 15, 2016). https://www.psychologytoday.com/blog/why-we-worry/201612/social-media-loneliness-and-anxiety-in-young-people.

Hale, Benjamin. "The History of Social Media: Social Networking Evolution!" History Cooperative, June 16, 2015. http://historycooperative.org/the-history-of-social-media/.

Khazan, Olga. "How Smartphones Hurt Sleep." *Atlantic* (February 24, 2015). https://www.theatlantic.com/health/archive/2015/02/how-smartphones-are-ruining-our-sleep/385792/.

Knapton, Sarah. "Facebook Users Have 155 Friends—But Would Trust Just Four in a Crisis." *Telegraph* (January 20, 2016). http://www.telegraph.co.uk/news/science/science-news/12108412/Facebook-users-have-155-friends-but-would-trust-just-four-in-a-crisis.html.

Larbi, Miranda. "Social Media Anxiety is a Real Thing and Here's What it's Like to Have it." *Metro* (November 11, 2016). http://metro.co.uk/2016/11/11/social-media-anxiety-is-a-real-thing-and-heres-what-its-like-to-have-it-6248947/.

Levitin, Daniel J. *The Organized Mind: Thinking Straight in the Age of Information Overload.* New York, NY: Dutton, 2014.

Maldonado, Marissa. "The Anxiety of Facebook." Psych Central, May 17, 2016. https://psychcentral.com/lib/the-anxiety-of-facebook/.

Murphy, Kate. "Do Your Friends Actually Like You?" *New York Times*, August 6, 2016. https://www.nytimes.com/2016/08/07/opinion/sunday/do-your-friends-actually-like-you.html?_r=0.

Real Time Statistics Project. "Internet Live Stats." Retrieved January 27, 2017. http://www.internetlivestats.com/.

Smith, Melinda, and Robert Segal. "Therapy for Anxiety Disorders." Help Guide, December 2016. https://www.helpguide.org/articles/anxiety/therapy-for-anxiety-disorders.htm.